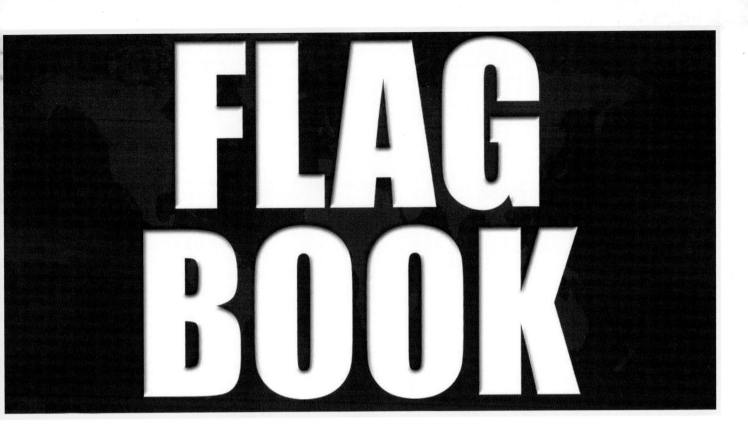

CONTENTS

THROUGH TIME

In ancient times, it was the flag that told one if the approaching individual was a friend or foe. The flag also helped a discouraged army to renew the fight with spirit.

CHINESE FLAG

Those battle flags were first devised by the Chinese and the Indians. It is believed that as far back as 1122 BC, the founder of China's Chou Dynasty travelled with a white-coloured flag as his emblem. The royal flag was identified with the prestige of the king's office and it was considered a crime to show it any disrespect. The fall of the flag would signify defeat for the king and, hence, its protection was entrusted to an able general. Standard motifs in Chinese flags included the blue dragon, the red bird and the white tiger.

INDIAN *DHVAJA*

Indian flags commonly featured a figure designed in golden shades and fringe, against a scarlet or green background. The shape was often triangular. The flags were usually mounted on chariots or elephants, especially during a battle.

ISLAMIC FLAG

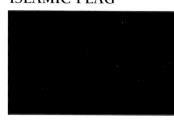

In contrast, Islamic flags were one plain colour – black, white, or red. This was because Islam disallowed the usage of any known image. In course of time, green, which was the colour of the 10th-century-AD Fatimid Dynasty, was adopted by Islam.

Europe took its own time to embrace the idea of the flag. In the Middle Ages, leaders began using the flag of their patron saint to represent their country – for instance, the Cross of St George (white with a red cross) was widely used in 13th-century England. The oldest European flags still in use are those with the Christian cross, which was widely used in the Crusades – military wars fought against Muslims in the 11th-13th centuries.

CROSS OF ST GEORGE

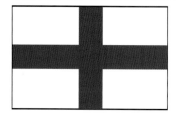

By the end of the Middle Ages, flags became the standard symbols of nations, cities, organisations and guilds. They also began to find uses for signalling as also for decoration and display. Special meanings came to be associated with particular types and colours of flags. The white flag has been used as a universal signal for peace. Similarly, the black flag became the symbol of pirates and later, of mourning.

KYRENIA CRUSADER FLAG

Over time, nations adopted flags to represent themselves. The colours and designs of these flags go back a long time – to the history, culture, values and struggles of a particular country and era.

The study of the various aspects of flags is known as vexillology (from the Latin *vexillum*, meaning 'banner'). Some sources assert it was the Roman Empire's *vexillum* that was the first 'true' flag.

ROMAN VEXILLUM

TYPES OF FLAGS

The colours in a flag follow a 'fixed and ordered pattern', and certainly cannot be altered as and when one wishes. A flag's colours usually have a history behind their adoption and bear distinct meanings. Flags are usually rectangular, though one sees flags in squares, pennants, swallowtails and other shapes too. The flag of Nepal is, in fact, a combination of two triangular forms!

Typically, designs on flags are crosses, stripes, stars and divisions of the surface (field) into bands. Flags are mainly distinguished by their respective national symbols. Flags may also feature different designs on each side, as can be seen on several flags of the U.S. states.

BORDER

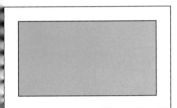

BICOLOUR

TRICOLOUR

QUARTERED

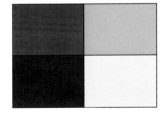

CROSS

SCANDINAVIAN CROSS

SALTIRE

COUPED CROSS

TRIANGLE

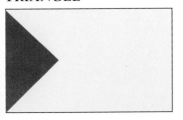

FIMBRIATION

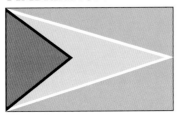

SERRATION

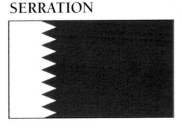

NORTH AND CENTRAL AMERICA

Canada, the second largest country in the world, takes up nearly two-fifths of the North American continent. Canada and the United States share a border about 8,895 kilometres (5,527 miles) long. Another country sharing a common border with the United States is Mexico. The world's largest island, Greenland, lies in the North Atlantic Ocean. Two-thirds of the island falls within the Arctic Circle and over 80 per cent of the surface is ice-capped.

BELIZE

Adopted on: September 21, 1981
Ratio: 3:5
Capital: Belmopan
Independence from the United Kingdom: September 21, 1981
What it means: The blue is the colour of the main political party, People's United Party (PUP), while the red represents the opposition United Democratic Party (UDP). The national coat of arms is featured in the middle.

CANADA

Adopted on: February 15, 1965
Ratio: 1:2
Capital: Ottawa
Independence (union of British North American colonies): July 1, 1867
What it means: Red and white are the national colours of Canada. The maple leaf at the centre is a national symbol.

COSTA RICA

Adopted on: September 29, 1848
Ratio: 3:5
Capital: San Jose
Independence from Spain: September 15, 1821
What it means: Blue and white are the original colours used by the United Provinces of Central America. The red, white and blue at the bottom are inspired by the French tricolour.

EL SALVADOR

Adopted on: May 17, 1912
Ratio: 4:7
Capital: San Salvador
Independence from Spain: September 15, 1821
What it means: Blue and white are the original colours used by the United Provinces of Central America. The coat of arms includes the national motto "God, union, liberty".

GREENLAND

Adopted on: June 21, 1985
Ratio: 2:3
Capital: Nuuk (Godthab)
Independence: none; self-governing part of the Kingdom of Denmark
What it means: The white stands for the island's ice cap and glaciers, while the red is symbolic of the fjords and the sun.

GUATEMALA

Adopted on: August 17, 1871
Ratio: 5:8
Capital: Guatemala
Independence from Spain: September 15, 1821
What it means: Blue and white are the original colours used by the United Provinces of Central America. The coat of arms features the national bird, the quetzal, as a symbol of liberty.

HONDURAS

Adopted on: February 16, 1866
Ratio: 1:2
Capital: Tegucigalpa
Independence from Spain: September 15, 1821
What it means: The colours and the five stars represent the United Provinces of Central America.

MEXICO

Adopted on: November 2, 1821
Ratio: 4:7
Capital: Mexico City
Independence from Spain: September 16, 1810
What it means: The colours are those of the national liberation army of Mexico. The coat of arms features the badge of Mexico City.

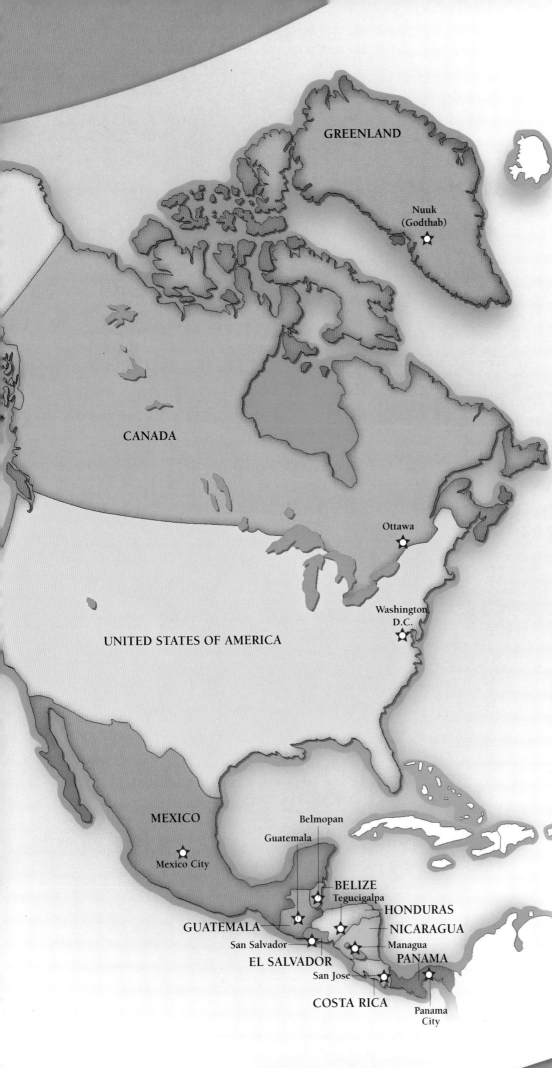

GREENLAND

Nuuk
(Godthab)

CANADA

Ottawa

Washington
D.C.

UNITED STATES OF AMERICA

MEXICO

Belmopan

Guatemala

Mexico City

BELIZE

Tegucigalpa

HONDURAS

GUATEMALA

NICARAGUA

San Salvador

Managua

EL SALVADOR

PANAMA

San Jose

COSTA RICA

Panama
City

NICARAGUA

Adopted on: September 4, 1908
Ratio: 3:5
Capital: Managua
Independence from Spain: September 15, 1821
What it means: The flag features the original colours used by the United Provinces of Central America. The five volcanoes in the coat of arms represent the five original Central American countries.

PANAMA

Adopted on: November 3, 1903
Ratio: 2:3
Capital: Panama City
Independence from Colombia: November 3, 1903; from Spain on November 28, 1821
What it means: Modelled on the U.S. flag, the red and blue originally represented the Liberal and Conservative parties, respectively. White symbolises peace.

UNITED STATES OF AMERICA

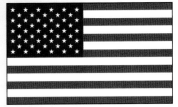

Adopted on: July 4, 1960
Ratio: 10:19
Capital: Washington, D.C.
Independence from Great Britain: July 4, 1776
What it means: The 50 stars represent the 50 states of the Union, while the 13 stripes stand for the 13 original states.

SOUTH
AMERICA

L ocated
between
the Pacific
and Atlantic oceans,
the continent of
South America is
roughly triangular
in shape. It is the
fourth largest
continent. Mount
Aconcagua in Argentina
is the continent's
highest point.
Argentina also boasts the
continent's lowest point –
the Valdés Peninsula.

GUYANA

Georgetown

Caracas

Paramaribo

VENEZUELA

Bogot

Cayenne

GUIANA
(FRENCH
GUIANA)

COLOMBIA

Quito

PERU

Lima

BRAZIL

Brasilia

ECUADOR

La Paz

BOLIVIA

PARAGUAY

Asuncion

CHILE

Santiago

Buenos Aires

URUGUAY

ARGENTINA

Montevideo

FALKLAND ISLANDS

Stanley

ARGENTINA

Adopted: 1812
Ratio: 1:2 and 9:14 on land; 2:3 at sea
Capital: Buenos Aires
Independence from Spain:
July 9, 1816
What it means: The 'Sun of May'
emblem refers to the events of May
1810, when, just before a battle,
General Belgrano, who designed the
flag, looked up and saw the clouds part
to show the blue sky and the shining sun.

BOLIVIA

Adopted: 1851
Ratio: 2:3
Capital: La Paz
Independence from Spain:
August 6, 1825
What it means: Red is said to
represent valour, yellow the
country's mineral wealth, and
green the fertile land.

BRAZIL

Adopted: 1889
Ratio: 7:10
Capital: Brasilia
Independence from Portugal: September 7, 1822
What it means: The green field is a symbol for Brazil's forests, while the yellow diamond represents gold. The blue disc features the motto 'Order and progress'.

CHILE

Adopted: 1817
Ratio: 2:3
Capital: Santiago
Independence from Spain: September 18, 1810
What it means: Blue is symbolic of the sky; white stands for the snow on the Andes Mountains; and red recalls the blood that was shed in the long freedom struggle.

COLOMBIA

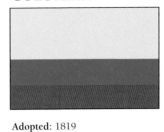

Adopted: 1819
Ratio: 2:3
Capital: Bogotá
Independence from Spain: July 20, 1810
What it means: Yellow is said to be symbolic of sovereignty and justice, blue of loyalty, and red of courage.

ECUADOR

Adopted: 1860
Ratio: 1:2
Capital: Quito
Independence from Spain: May 24, 1822
What it means: The colours are those of the tricolour flown by the South American revolutionary Francisco de Miranda.

FALKLAND ISLANDS

Adopted: 1948
Ratio: 1:2
Capital: Stanley
Independence: None; self-governing territory of the United Kingdom
What it means: The ram featured in the national coat of arms represents the islands' sheep industry. The U.K. flag is incorporated on the hoist side.

FRENCH GUIANA

Adopted: --
Ratio: 2:3
Capital: Cayenne
Independence: None; overseas department of France
What it means: Uses the flag of France.

GUYANA

Adopted: 1966
Ratio: 3:5 on land; 1:2 at sea
Capital: Georgetown
Independence from the United Kingdom: May 26, 1966
What it means: The yellow triangle symbolises bright future, red, the people's zeal in building the nation, and black, determination.

PARAGUAY

Adopted: 1842
Ratio: 3:5
Capital: Asuncion
Independence from Spain: May 14, 1811
What it means: The coat of arms depict the 'Star of May', a symbol of freedom. The treasury seal on the other side has the motto 'Peace and justice'.

PERU

Adopted: 1825
Ratio: 2:3
Capital: Lima
Independence from Spain: July 28, 1821
What it means: Red and white are associated with the ancient Inca people, who ruled Peru for centuries. The coat of arms is featured only when the government uses the flag.

SURINAME

Adopted: 1975
Ratio: 2:3
Capital: Paramaribo
Independence from the Netherlands: November 25, 1975
What it means: The green stripes are symbolic of the country's forests; white of justice and freedom; and red of the spirit of a new nation. The star represents unity and hope.

URUGUAY

Adopted: 1830
Ratio: 2:3
Capital: Montevideo
Independence from Brazil: August 25, 1825
What it means: The nine stripes are for the nine original departments of the republic. Like several other South American countries, the Uruguay flag too features the 'Sun of May'.

VENEZUELA

Adopted: 1836
Ratio: 2:3
Capital: Caracas
Independence from Spain: July 5, 1811
What it means: The arc of seven stars represent the original seven provinces that supported the independence movement.

THE CARIBBEAN

The Caribbean is a group of islands in the Caribbean Sea. Alternatively known as the West Indies, it comprises Anguilla, Antigua and Barbuda, Cayman Islands, the British Virgin Islands, the Bahamas, Dominica, Guadeloupe, Grenada and Montserrat.

THE BAHAMAS — Nassau

TURKS AND CAICOS ISLANDS — Grand Turk

PUERTO RICO

Havana

CUBA

CAYMAN ISLANDS — George Town

HAITI — Port-au-Prince

DOMINICAN REPUBLIC — Santo Domingo

San Juan

JAMAICA — Kingston

ANTIGUA AND BARBUDA

Adopted: 1967
Ratio: About 2:3
Capital: Saint John's
Independence from the United Kingdom: November 1, 1981
What it means: The V shape in the centre stands for victory, while the sun symbolises the dawn of a new era.

THE BAHAMAS

Adopted: 1973
Ratio: 1:2
Capital: Nassau
Independence from the United Kingdom: July 10, 1973
What it means: The aquamarine stripes are for the waters around the islands; the yellow for the sandy beaches; and the black triangle for the strength of the people.

BARBADOS

Adopted: 1966
Ratio: 2:3
Capital: Bridgetown
Independence from the United Kingdom: November 30, 1966
What it means: The blue-yellow-blue stripes stand for sea, sand and sky. The trident head is symbolic of the nation's break from its colonial history.

CAYMAN ISLANDS

Adopted: 1959
Ratio: 1:2
Capital: George Town
Independence: None; overseas territory of the United Kingdom
What it means: The three stars in the coat of arms represent the three main islands, while the pineapple and the turtle stand for the flora and fauna.

CUBA

Adopted: 1902
Ratio: 1:2
Capital: Havana
Independence from Spain: December 10, 1898
What it means: The red triangle is said to be a symbol for equality, and the white star in it for independence.

DOMINICA

Adopted: 1978
Ratio: 1:2
Capital: Roseau
Independence from the United Kingdom: November 3, 1978
What it means: The yellow-white-black cross represents the island's original inhabitants. The ring of 10 stars represents the 10 parishes.

DOMINICAN REPUBLIC

Adopted: 1844
Ratio: 5:8
Capital: Santo Domingo
Independence from Haiti:
February 27, 1844
What it means: The white
cross represents faith. When
used officially, the flag features
the coat of arms bearing the
flag, the Holy Bible and a cross.

GRENADA

Adopted: 1974
Ratio: 3:5
Capital: Saint George's
Independence from the
United Kingdom:
February 7, 1974
What it means: The outer stars
represent the six parishes and
the central star, the capital.

GUADELOUPE

Adopted: --
Ratio: 2:3
Capital: Basse-Terre
Independence: None; overseas
department of France
What it means: The flag of
France is used.

HAITI

Adopted: 1803
Ratio: 3:5
Capital: Port-au-Prince
Independence from France:
January 1, 1804
What it means: The blue and
red are taken from the French
tricolour. The coat of arms is
inscribed with the motto
'Union makes strength'.

ANTIGUA
AND
BARBUDA

Saint John's

asseterre
AINT
KITTS
ND
NEVIS

DOMINICA
Roseau

SAINT LUCIA

GRENADA
Saint George's

ARBADOS Bridgetown
TRINIDAD Port-of-Spain
AND TOBAGO

Kingstown

Castries

SAINT
VINCENT
AND THE
GRENADINES

JAMAICA

Adopted: 1962
Ratio: 1:2
Capital: Kingston
Independence from the United
Kingdom: August 6, 1962
What it means: the black,
yellow and green represent,
respectively, the difficulties
suffered by the nation, the
shining sun, and the fertile land.

PUERTO RICO

Adopted: 1922
Ratio: 1:2
Capital: San Juan
Independence: None; self-
governing commonwealth
associated with the United States
What it means: The white
stripes symbolise liberty, and
the red ones and the triangle,
the legislative, executive and
judicial branches of the state.

SAINT KITTS AND NEVIS

Adopted: 1983
Ratio: About 2:3
Capital: Basseterre
Independence from the
United Kingdom: September
19, 1983
What it means: The green
triangle represents land and
the red one, years of freedom
struggle. The black symbolises
the islands' African heritage.

SAINT LUCIA

Adopted: 1967
Ratio: 1:2
Capital: Castries
Independence from the
United Kingdom:
February 22, 1979
What it means: The blue is for
the Caribbean Sea. The
triangles are for the famous
twin peaks of the Pitons.

SAINT VINCENT AND THE GRENADINES

Adopted: 1985
Ratio: 2:3
Capital: Kingstown
Independence from the United
Kingdom: October 27, 1979
What it means: The green
diamonds represent the 'Gems
of the Antilles', as the islands
are known. The V shape refers
to the first alphabet in Vincent.

TRINIDAD AND TOBAGO

Adopted: 1962
Ratio: 3:5
Capital: Port-of-Spain
Independence from the United
Kingdom: August 31, 1962
What it means: The white
stripes symbolise the sea.
Red represents the vitality
of the people and black,
their strength.

WESTERN EUROPE

Western Europe is made up of a widely varying landscape – from Spain, located at the intersection of Europe and Africa, to the island nation of Iceland, which has an abundance of glaciers and geysers. The 'emerald isle' of Ireland boasts an Atlantic coastline with a 3,200-kilometre-(2,000-mile)-wide stretch of ocean.

ANDORRA

Adopted: 1866
Ratio: 2:3
Capital: Andorra la Vella
Independence: 1278
What it means: The colours are taken from the flags of France and Spain, which have joint jurisdiction over the principality. The Andorran coat of arms is featured in the centre.

BELGIUM

Adopted: 1831
Ratio: 13:15
Capital: Brussels
Independence from the Netherlands: October 4, 1830
What it means: The colours have been taken from the national coat of arms – black from the shield, gold from the lion, and red from the lion's claws and tongue.

FRANCE

Adopted: 1794
Ratio: 2:3
Capital: Paris
Independence: 486
What it means: The colours stand for the ideals of the 1789 French Revolution – liberty, equality and fraternity.

IRELAND

Adopted: 1919
Ratio: 1:2
Capital: Dublin
Independence from the United Kingdom: December 6, 1921
What it means: Green is symbolic of the Roman Catholics, orange of the Protestants, and white of peace between the two sects.

ICELAND

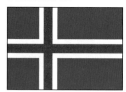

Adopted: 1915
Ratio: 18:25
Capital: Reykjavik
Independence from Denmark: June 17, 1944
What it means: The red is thought to symbolise the volcanoes in the island country. White is for snow and ice, and blue is the bordering Atlantic Ocean. The cross design is based on the Danish flag.

ITALY

Adopted: 1919
Ratio: 2:3
Capital: Rome
Independence (Kingdom of Italy proclaimed): March 17, 1861
What it means: One legend has it that the green in the flag was used since it was the favourite colour of Napoleon. However, the green and the white might also have been based on the uniforms of the militia of Milan, Italy.

LUXEMBOURG

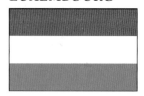

Adopted: 1972
Ratio: 3:5
Capital: Luxembourg
Independence from the Netherlands: 1839
What it means: The colours go back to the 13th-century coat of arms used by the grand duke.

MALTA

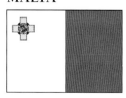

Adopted: 1964
Ratio: 2:3
Capital: Valletta
Independence from the United Kingdom: September 21, 1964
What it means: The colours were taken from the badge used by the Knights of Malta.

MONACO

Adopted: 1881
Ratio: 4:5
Capital: Monaco
Independence (the House of Grimaldi begins its rule): 1419
What it means: The red and white are the heraldic colours of the House of Grimaldi.

NETHERLANDS, THE

Adopted: 1937
Ratio: 2:3
Capital: Amsterdam
Independence: January 23, 1579
What it means: The colours were originally taken from the livery colours of William of Orange, a Dutch prince (the orange was later replaced by red).

PORTUGAL

Adopted: 1911
Ratio: 2:3
Capital: Lisbon
Independence (Kingdom of Portugal recognized): 1143
What it means: Green represents the Portuguese explorer, King Henry the Navigator. Red was the colour of the revolutionary flag. The central shield is symbolic of the country's history of ocean exploration.

SAN MARINO

Adopted: 1862
Ratio: 3:4
Capital: San Marino
Independence (republic founded): September 3, 301
What it means: White is symbolic of the snow on Mount Titano, the country's highest point, and blue symbolises the sky.

ICELAND
Reykjavik

IRELAND
Dublin

UNITED KINGDOM
London

NETHERLANDS
Amsterdam

BELGIUM
Brussels

LUXEMBOURG
Luxembourg

SWISS CONFEDERATION
Bern

ITALIAN REPUBLIC
Rome

SAN MARINO
San Marino

PORTUGUESE REPUBLIC
Lisbon

SPAIN
Madrid

ANDORRA
Andorra la Vella

FRENCH REPUBLIC
Paris

MONACO
Monaco

VATICAN CITY
Vatican City

Valletta MALTA

SPAIN

Adopted: 1927
Ratio: 2:3
Capital: Madrid
Independence (unification of several independent kingdoms): 1492
What it means: Red and yellow are the original colours of the coat of arms of the Castile and Aragon regions.

SWITZERLAND

Adopted: 1889
Ratio: Square in proportion
Capital: Bern
Independence (founding of the confederation): August 1, 1291
What it means: The design is based on the war flag used by the Holy Roman Empire.

UNITED KINGDOM

Adopted: 1801
Ratio: 1:2
Capital: London
Independence (current name of the United Kingdom of Great Britain and Northern Ireland adopted): 1927
What it means: The design features three crosses – of St George (England), St Andrew (Scotland) and St Patrick (Ireland).

VATICAN CITY

Adopted: 1929
Ratio: Square in proportion
Capital: Vatican City
Independence from Italy: February 11, 1929
What it means: The colours are those of the keys of St Peter's. The emblem itself features the keys upholding the papal crown.

CENTRAL EUROPE

Central Europe is largely made up of landlocked territories – Slovenia being exception. Slovenia has been shaped by limestone plateaus, ridges, caves, underground rivers, valleys and the steep Alpine peaks. There is also a short coastal strip to its southwest. The landscape of Slovakia is marked by the Western Carpathian Mountains. The Alps forms a natural and majestic barrier for the countries of Germany and Austria.

AUSTRIA

Adopted: 1945
Ratio: 2:3
Capital: Vienna
Independence (proclaimed republic): November 12, 1918
What it means: The colours red and white have long been associated with the Austrian legend of the Battle of Acre and the blood-stained white tunic of the war hero, Luitpold V of Badenberg.

CZECH REPUBLIC

Adopted: 1920
Ratio: 2:3
Capital: Prague
Independence : January 1, 1993 (Czechoslovakia split into the Czech Republic and Slovakia)
What it means: The stripes are the herladic colours of Bohemia, which make up a large part of the Czech Republic. The blue of the isosceles triangle was used to represent the state of Moravia in the republic.

SWEDEN

FINLA

NORWAY

Oslo

Helsinki

Stockholm

DENMARK
Copenhagen

Berlin

Warsaw

GERMANY

POLAND

Prague

CZECH
REPUBLIC

Vaduz

Bratislava

Vienna

LIECHTENSTEIN

AUSTRIA

SLOVAK REPUBLIC

SLOVENIA

Ljubljana

DENMARK

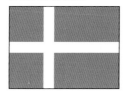

Adopted in: 1625 (oldest European flag)
Ratio: 28:34 (can be extended to 37)
Capital: Copenhagen
Independence (became a constitutional monarchy): June 5, 1849
What it means: The flag (Dannebrog) is claimed to be a token from the Pope given at the time of the Crusades. The cross design (Scandinavian Cross) was later adopted by other regional flags.

FINLAND

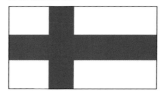

Adopted: 1918
Ratio: 11:18
Capital: Helsinki
Independence from Russia: December 6, 1917
What it means: The blue is for the thousands of lakes in Finland, and the white for the snow. When flown by the government, the flag has the coat of arms featuring a lion.

GERMANY

Adopted: 1949
Ratio: 3:5
Capital: Berlin
Independence (federal republic proclaimed): May 23, 1949
What it means: The colours were taken after the uniforms of German soldiers who fought in the Napoleonic Wars (1804-1815).

LIECHTENSTEIN

Adopted: 1937
Ratio: 3:5
Capital: Vaduz
Independence from the Holy Roman Empire: July 12, 1806
What it means: The crown symbolises the independence of the principality. Blue and red respectively stand for the sky and the evening fires at homes.

NORWAY

Adopted: 1821
Ratio: 8:11
Capital: Oslo
Independence (union with Sweden declared dissolved): June 7, 1905
What it means: The tricolour is a symbol of liberty, and influenced by the French, U.K. and U.S. flags. The cross takes after the design of the Danish and Swedish flags.

POLAND

Adopted: 1919
Ratio: 5:8
Capital: Warsaw
Independence: November 11, 1918
What it means: The white and red have traditionally been associated with Poland's coat of arms.

SLOVENIA

Adopted: 1836
Ratio: 1:2
Capital: Ljubljana
Independence from Yugoslavia: June 25, 1991
What it means: The colours are the traditional pan-Slavic colours used on the flags of the Slavic peoples of Europe. The coat of arms is said to be based on the one used by the duchy of Celje.

SWEDEN

Adopted: 1906
Ratio: 5:8
Capital: Stockholm
Independence: June 6, 1523
What it means: The yellow and blue colours are those of the national coat of arms. The cross, again, is designed after the Danish flag.

SLOVAKIA

Adopted: 1992
Ratio: 2:3
Capital: Bratislava
ndependence (Czechoslovakia split into the Czech Republic and Slovakia): January 1, 1993
What it means: The flag features the traditional pan-Slavic colours.

EASTERN EUROPE

Geographically, Eastern Europe is marked as the region extending from the Ural and Caucasus mountains in the east to the western border of Russia. Nearly all the countries in this region gained independence only in the 20th century. Russia is the world's largest country, occupying about double the area of the United States!

ALBANIA

Adopted on: April 7, 1992
Ratio: 5:7
Capital: Tiranë
Independence from Ottoman Empire: November 28, 1912
What it means: The double-headed black eagle represents an incident when a native prince of the 15th century successfully raised his red-coloured flag bearing the eagle, in rebellion against the Turks.

GREECE

Adopted: 1822
Ratio: 2:3
Capital: Athens
Independence from the Ottoman Empire: 1829
What it means: The nine stripes are taken for the nine syllables in the battle cry for independence, translated as "Freedom or death". The cross symbolises Greek religious faith.

BOSNIA AND HERZEGOVINA

Adopted: February 1998
Ratio: 1:2
Capital: Sarajevo
Independence from Yugoslavia; declared: March 3, 1992
What it means: The gold shield is from the arms of the great Bosnian ruler Stephen Tvrtho (reigned 1377-91).

HUNGARY

Adopted on: October 1, 1957
Ratio: 2:3
Capital: Budapest
Independence (unification by King Stephen I): 1001
What it means: Designed after the French tricolour. The red stands for strength, green for hope, and white for faithfulness.

BELARUS

Adopted: 1995
Ratio: 1:2
Capital: Minsk
Independence (from Soviet Union): August 25, 1991
What it means: The red is thought to signify the blood shed by the patriots of Belarus. The red embroidered pattern is Belarusian national ornamentation.

BULGARIA

Adopted: 1990
Ratio: 3:5
Capital: Sofia
Independence (declared; from Ottoman Empire): September 22, 1908
What it means: The white stands for peace, love and freedom; the green for the country's agricultural resources; and the red for the independence movement and the courage of the freedom fighters.

CROATIA

Adopted: 1990
Ratio: 1:2
Capital: Zagreb
Independence from Yugoslavia: June 25, 1991
What it means: The stripes feature the traditional Croatian colours. The national coat of arms in the middle has a main shield with five shields on top. The checkerboard design is an ancient symbol of the Croatian kings.

ESTONIA

Adopted: 1990
Ratio: 7:11
Capital: Tallinn
Independence (recognised; from Soviet Union): August 20, 1991
What it means: The blue is a symbol of faith as well as the sky, seas and lakes; black of historic suppression as well as the soil; and white represents virtue, enlightenment and snow, as also for the country's freedom struggle.

LATVIA

Adopted: 1900
Ratio: 1:2
Capital: Riga
Independence (recognised; from Soviet Union): August 21, 1991
What it means: The flag represents a legend about a Latvian tribal leader who was wrapped in a white cloth after he was injured in a battle. A part of the cloth became stained with his blood, while the rest remained white.

RUSSIA

LITHUANIA

Adopted: 1989
Ratio: 1:2
Capital: Vilnius
Independence (recognised; from Soviet Union): September 6, 1991
What it means: The yellow symbolises ripening wheat and freedom from want or need; green signifies hope and also represents the country's forests; and red stands for patriotism and right to freedom.

MOLDOVA

Adopted: 1990
Ratio: 1:2
Capital: Chisinau
Independence (from Soviet Union): August 27, 1991
What it means: The flag reflects the tricolour of Romania, of which Moldova was once a part of. The emblem is a Roman eagle carrying a yellow cross in its beak, a green olive branch and a yellow sceptre in its talons.

ROMANIA

Adopted: 1989
Ratio: 2:3
Capital: Bucharest
Independence from Turkey: May 9, 1877
What it means: The tricolour goes back to Romania's past association with Moldova and Wallachia. The flag came into existence when Moldova and Wallachia united to form Romania, but that flag had horizontal stripes.

RUSSIA

Adopted: 1991
Ratio: 2:3
Capital: Moscow
Independence (from Soviet Union): August 24, 1991
What it means: The white represents nobility, blue, truthfulness and commitment and red, valour and love. The flag was adopted by the Russian Czar, Peter the Great, who was impressed by the Dutch tricolour.

UKRAINE

Adopted: 1991
Ratio: 2:3
Capital: Kiev (Kyyiv)
Independence (from Soviet Union): August 24, 1991
What it means: The colours symbolise blue skies over golden wheat fields of the Steppes plains.

MACEDONIA

Adopted on: October 5, 1995
Ratio: 1:2
Capital: Skopje
Independence from Yugoslavia: September 8, 1991
What it means: The design of the 'golden sun' finds mention in the country's national anthem. Red is a traditional colour of Macedonia.

SERBIA AND MONTENEGRO

Adopted: 1992
Ratio: 1:2
Capital: Belgrade
Independence (Federal Republic of Yugoslavia, now Serbia and Montenegro, formed): April 27, 1992
What it means: The colours stand for Slavic unity and independence.

THE MIDDLE EAST

D eserts define much of the Middle East landscape. Iran is largely a central desert plateau – surrounded by soaring mountain ranges. Nearly two-fifths of Iraq too consists of desert. Kuwait and Qatar, again, comprises deserts. Saudi Arabia is largely uninhabited and includes the world's largest sand area, the Rub' al-Khali (the Empty Quarter). Turkey is one of the few exceptions – it is primarily mountainous and boasts coastlines along the Aegean, the Mediterranean and the Black seas.

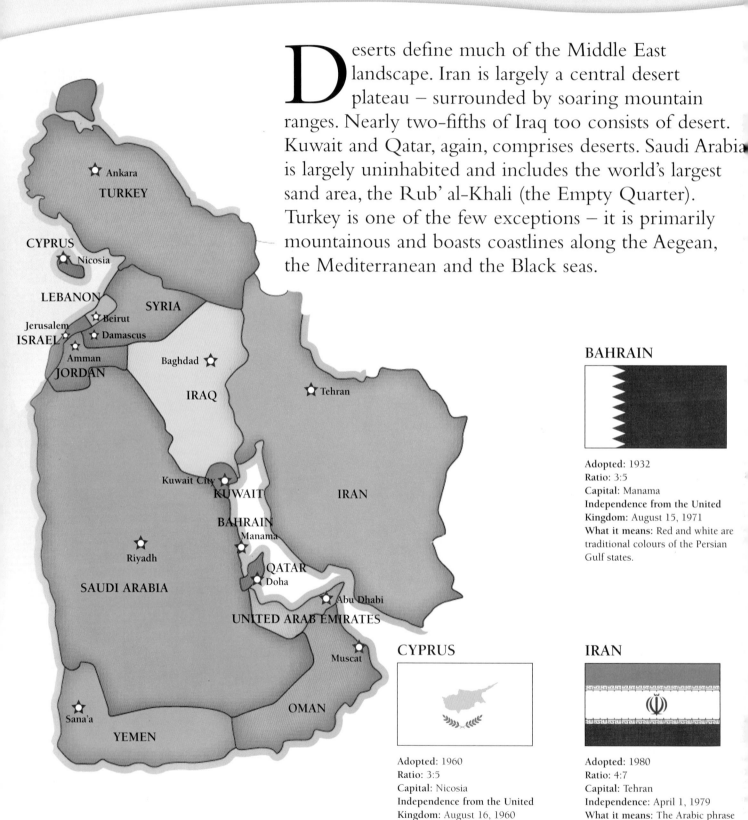

BAHRAIN

Adopted: 1932
Ratio: 3:5
Capital: Manama
Independence from the United Kingdom: August 15, 1971
What it means: Red and white are traditional colours of the Persian Gulf states.

CYPRUS

Adopted: 1960
Ratio: 3:5
Capital: Nicosia
Independence from the United Kingdom: August 16, 1960
What it means: The olive branches symbolise the hope for peace between the island's Greek and Turkish communities. The copper-coloured outline of the island's map is for its name, which is Greek for 'copper'.

IRAN

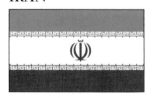

Adopted: 1980
Ratio: 4:7
Capital: Tehran
Independence: April 1, 1979
What it means: The Arabic phrase *Allahu Akbar* ('God is great') is repeated 22 times along the edges of the green and red bands. The coat of arms can be taken as a stylised Arabic representation of the word Allah.

IRAQ

Adopted: 1991
Ratio: 1:2
Capital: Baghdad
Independence from League of Nations mandate under British control: October 3, 1932
What it means: The phrase *Allahu akbar* is incorporated between the stars. Red, green, white and black are the traditional colours across the Arab world.

ISRAEL

Adopted: 1948
Ratio: 8:11
Capital: Jerusalem
Independence from League of Nations mandate under British control: May 14, 1948
What it means: The six-pointed star is known as the Magen David (Star of David) and is supposed to symbolise King David's shield. Blue and white are taken from the traditional Jewish prayer shawl.

JORDAN

Adopted: 1928
Ratio: 1:2
Capital: Amman
Independence from League of Nations mandate under British control: May 25, 1946
What it means: The hoist-side triangle is symbolic of the Great Arab Revolt of 1916. The seven-pointed star signify the opening seven verses of the Qur'an.

KUWAIT

Adopted: 1961
Ratio: 1:2
Capital: Kuwait City
Independence from the United Kingdom: June 19, 1961
What it means: Green stands for the fertile land, white for purity, red for the blood of the enemy, and black for the enemy's defeat.

LEBANON

Adopted: 1943
Ratio: 2:3
Capital: Beirut
Independence from League of Nations mandate under French control November 22, 1943
What it means: The cedar tree has traditionally been a symbol for immortality, strength and wealth.

OMAN

Adopted: 1995
Ratio: Usually 1:2
Capital: Muscat
Independence (the Portuguese were driven out): 1650
What it means: The coat of arms is a dagger in its sheath superimposed on two crossed swords in their holders

QATAR

Adopted: 1949
Ratio: 11:28
Capital: Doha (Ad-Dawhah)
Independence from the United Kingdom: September 3, 1971
What it means: It is said that the original red dye on the flag got altered into maroon in the Qatar sun! The flag looks similar to that of Bahrain, since Qatar was once a part of Bahrain.

SAUDI ARABIA

Adopted: 1973
Ratio: 2:3
Capital: Riyadh
Independence (unification of the kingdom): September 23, 1932
What it means: Green is a traditional colour in Islamic flags. The Arabic inscription reads: "There is no god but Allah; Muhammad is the prophet of God."

SYRIA

Adopted: 1980
Ratio: 2:3
Capital: Damascus
Independence from League of Nations mandate under French control: April 17, 1946
What it means: The stars represent Syria and Egypt, which were briefly united in 1958 to form the United Arab Republic. The colours are based on the Arab Liberation Flag.

TURKEY

Adopted: 1936
Ratio: Approximately 2:3
Capital: Ankara
Independence (republic declared): October 29, 1923
What it means: The crescent and the star are symbols of Islam.

UNITED ARAB EMIRATES

Adopted: 1971
Ratio: 1:2
Capital: Abu Dhabi
Independence ffrom the United Kingdom: December 2, 1971
What it means: Incorporates the traditional Arab colours of unity and nationalism.

YEMEN

Adopted: 1990
Ratio: 2:3
Capital: Sana'a
Independence (republic declared with the union of North Yemen and South Yemen): May 22, 1990
What it means: The flag was adopted upon the unification of North and South Yemen.

WESTERN AND SOUTHERN
ASIA

Afghanistan, Armenia, Bhutan and Nepal in Western Asia are landlocked countries. Rugged mountains make for some of the world's most difficult terrains in the rest of this region.

GEORGIA
T'bilisi
Yerevan
ARMENIA
AZERBAIJAN
Baku
Ashgabat
TURKMENISTAN
Astana
KAZAKHSTAN
UZBEKISTAN
Tashkent
Bishkek
KYRGYZSTAN
Dushanbe
TAJIKISTAN
Kabul
AFGHANISTAN
Islamabad
PAKISTAN
New Delhi
NEPAL
Kathmandu
BHUTAN
Thimphu
Dhaka
BANGLADESH
INDIA
MALDIVES
Male
SRI LANKA
Colombo

AFGHANISTAN

Adopted: 2002
Ratio: 1:2
Capital: Kabul
Independence (from U.K. control over foreign affairs): August 19, 1919
What it means: The coat of arms found in the centre of the flag incorporates a mosque encircled by sheaves of wheat and an Islamic inscription.

ARMENIA

Adopted: 1990
Ratio: 1:2
Capital: Yerevan
Independence (from Soviet Union): September 21, 1991
What it means: Red is said to be symbolic of the blood shed by Armenians in their freedom struggle; blue of their skies and hope; and orange of hard work.

AZERBAIJAN

Adopted: 1991
Ratio: 1:2
Capital: Baku
Independence (from Soviet Union): August 30, 1991
What it means: The crescent and the star are symbols of Islam. The eight-pointed stars are thought to represent the eight traditional Turkic peoples.

BANGLADESH

Adopted: 1972
Ratio: 6:10
Capital: Dhaka
Independence (from Pakistan): March 26, 1971
What it means: The disc symbolises the 'rising sun of a new country,' and the colour red symbolises the blood that was shed in the struggle for independence.

BHUTAN

Adopted: 1969
Ratio: 2:3
Capital: Thimphu
Independence from India:
August 8, 1949
What it means: The 'thunder' dragon at the centre is the country's national emblem. White is a symbol of purity and loyalty, yellow of the king's power and orange of Buddhist religious practices and monastries.

GEORGIA

Adopted: 2004
Ratio: 2:3
Capital: T'bilisi
Independence from Soviet Union:
April 9, 1991
What it means: The central cross connects all four sides of the flag, with each four corner featuring the bolnur-katskhuri crosses. The five-cross theme dates back to the 14th century.

INDIA

Adopted: 1947
Ratio: 2:3
Capital: New Delhi
Independence (from the United Kingdom): August 15, 1947
What it means: The orange (courage and sacrifice), white (peace and truth) and green (faith and chivalry) flag features a 24-spoked Buddhist charka ('Wheel of the Law') at the centre. This wheel stands for non-violence.

KAZAKHSTAN

Adopted: June 4, 1992
Ratio: Approximately 1:2
Capital: Astana
Independence from the Soviet Union:
December 16, 1991
What it means: Traditional Kazakh ornamentation is featured on the hoist side. A golden steppe eagle in flight is depicted below the shining sun.

KYRGYZSTAN

Adopted on: March 3, 1992
Ratio: Approximately 3:5
Capital: Bishkek
Independence from the Soviet Union:
August 31, 1991
What it means: The red background is said to have been adopted from the flag carried by the famed Kyrgyz hero, Manas the Noble. The 40 rays of the sun are symbolic of the tribes that the leader helped unite to form the nation.

MALDIVES

Adopted: 1965
Ratio: 2:3
Capital: Male
Independence (from the United Kingdom): July 26, 1965
What it means: Red was the colour of the country's first flag. The green panel with a crescent is symbolic of Islam.

NEPAL

Adopted: 1962
Ratio: 4:3
Capital: Kathmandu
Independence (unified by Prithvi Narayan Shah): 1768
What it means: Two triangles overlap, one with a crescent moon and the other bearing a 12-pointed sun. Red is the colour of the national flower, the rhododendron. The blue stands for peace.

PAKISTAN

Adopted: 1947
Ratio: 2:3
Capital: Islamabad
Independence (from the United Kingdom): August 14, 1947
What it means: The traditional symbols of Islam are used. The white represents the country's non-Muslim population. The star is symbolic of knowledge and light, and the crescent, of progress.

SRI LANKA

Adopted: 1978
Ratio: 1:2
Capital: Colombo
Independence (from the United Kingdom): February 4, 1948
What it means: The dark-red rectangle has a lion holding a sword, and four bo leaves, associated with Buddhism, at the corners. The thinner green and orange panels represent the minority Islamic and Tamil communities.

TAJIKISTAN

Adopted on: November 24, 1992
Ratio: 1:2
Capital: Dushanbe
Independence from Soviet Union:
September 9, 1991
What it means: The centred crown and the arc of seven gold stars are said to symbolise unity among the country's various social classes.

TURKMENISTAN

Adopted on: February 19, 1997
Ratio: 1:2
Capital: Ashgabat
Independence from the Soviet Union:
October 27, 1991
What it means: The five carpet motifs on the hoist-side are representative of the country's rich, traditional carpet industry.

UZBEKISTAN

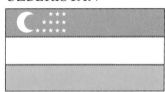

Adopted on: November 18, 1991
Ratio: Approximately 1:2
Capital: Tashkent
Independence from the Soviet Union:
September 1, 1991
What it means: The 12 stars are for the 12 months in a year as well as for the constellations in the zodiac.

EAST AND SOUTHEAST
ASIA

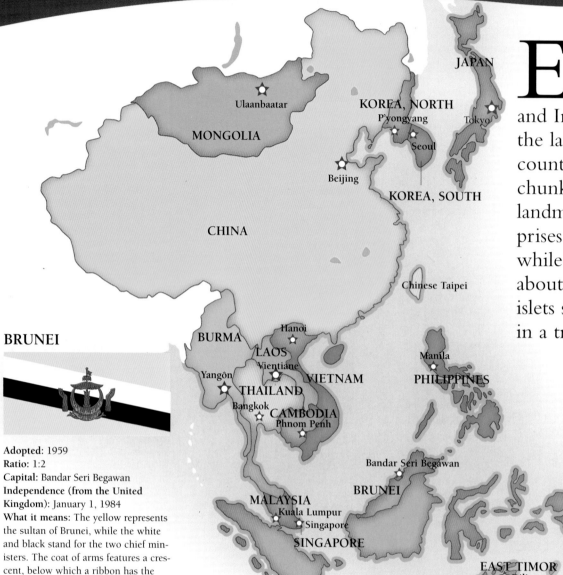

E ast and Southeast Asia are located between the Pacifi and Indian oceans. China the largest of the Asian countries, occupy a majo chunk of the East Asian landmass. Indonesia comprises over 13,600 islands while Philippines has about 7,100 islands and islets spreading out in a triangle.

BRUNEI

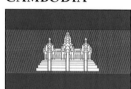

Adopted: 1959
Ratio: 1:2
Capital: Bandar Seri Begawan
Independence (from the United Kingdom): January 1, 1984
What it means: The yellow represents the sultan of Brunei, while the white and black stand for the two chief ministers. The coat of arms features a crescent, below which a ribbon has the inscription 'Brunei, abode of peace'.

CAMBODIA

Adopted: 1993
Ratio: 2:3
Capital: Phnom Penh
Independence from France: November 9, 1953
What it means: Red and blue are the country's traditional colours. At the centre is the three-towered temple complex of Angkor Wat, making it the only national flag to feature a building.

CHINA

Adopted: 1949
Ratio: 2:3
Capital: Beijing
Independence (People's Republic established): October 1, 1949
What it means: Red, besides being the Chinese traditional colour, represents the communist revolution. The large star stands for the Chinese Communist Party, with the other four smaller ones denoting the four social classes.

EAST TIMOR

Adopted: 2002
Ratio: 1:2
Capital: Dili
Independence (recognised; from Portugal): May 20, 2002
What it means: The colour yellow represents centuries of colonial repression, black stands for uncertainities that need to be overcome and red is for freedom struggle. The white star is the 'light that guides'.

INDONESIA

Adopted: 1945
Ratio: 2:3
Capital: Jakarta
Independence (declared; from the Netherlands): August 17, 1945
What it means: The flag goes back to the 13th century, when the Majapahit Empire used a similar flag. Indonesian consider the traditional colours of red (courage) and white (honesty) holy.

APAN

Adopted: 1870
Ratio: 2:3
Capital: Tokyo
Independence (traditional founding):
60 BC
What it means: The red disc of the
un (Hinomaru) is a traditional
apanese symbol. The white stands
or honesty and purity.

KOREA, NORTH

Adopted: 1948
Ratio: 1:2
Capital: P'yongyang
Independence (from Japan):
August 15, 1945
What it means: The red stripe and the
star represent the communist ideology.
The blue and white stripes, respectively,
symbolise peace and purity.

KOREA, SOUTH

Adopted: 1950
Ratio: 2:3
Capital: Seoul
Independence (from Japan):
August 15, 1945
What it means: The flag is called
Iaegukki. The yin-yang symbol stands
for unity. The four sets of black bars
represent sun, moon, earth and heaven.

LAOS

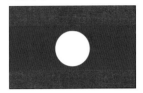

Adopted: 1975
Ratio: 2:3
Capital: Vientiane
Independence (from France):
July 19, 1949
What it means: The white disc on
a blue field is believed to be symbolic
of the moon glowing over the
Mekong River.

MALAYSIA

Adopted: 1963
Ratio: 1:2
Capital: Kuala Lumpur
**Independence (from the United
Kingdom):** August 31, 1957
What it means: The 14 stripes and 14
points of the star represent the original
14 states of Malaysia. Since Singapore
eft the federation in 1965, the 14th
stripe and point is said to represent
the Malaysian government.

MONGOLIA

Adopted: 1940
Ratio: 1:2
Capital: Ulaanbaatar
Independence (from China):
July 11, 1921
What it means: The sky blue is
Mongolia's national colour. The tradi-
tional emblem of *soyonbo* is featured
in the red bar on the
hoist side.

BURMA

Adopted: 1974
Ratio: 5:9
Capital: Yangôn
**Independence (from the United
Kingdom):** January 4, 1948
What it means: The 14 stars are for
the 14 states and other divisions of the
country. These encircle a cogwheel
framing a stalk of rice, a symbol of the
peasant force and the union of industry and agriculture.

PHILIPPINES, THE

Adopted: 1898
Ratio: Usually 1:2
Capital: Manila
Independence (from Spain): June 12,
1898
What it means: The three stars are for
Luzon, Mindanao and Visayan. The
sun symbolises independence, and its
eight rays, the provinces that rose
against the Spanish rule. Blue and red
stand for patriotism and courage.

SINGAPORE

Adopted: 1959
Ratio: 2:3
Capital: Singapore
**Independence (from Malaysian
Federation):** August 9, 1965
What it means: The white crescent
is symbolic of the young nation. The
five stars stand for democracy, peace,
progress, justice and equality. Red signifies universal brotherhood and white,
purity and virtue.

THAILAND

Adopted: 1917
Ratio: 2:3
Capital: Bangkok
Independence (traditional founding):
1238
What it means: The common symbol-
isms are – red for the blood sacrificed
by the people for their country, white
for the purity of Buddhism, and blue
for the monarchy.

VIETNAM

Adopted: 1955
Ratio: 2:3
Capital: Hanoi
Independence (from France):
September 2, 1945
What it means: The main classes of
workers are represented by the five
points of the star.

NORTH AND WEST AFRICA

The largest desert in the world, the Sahara, spreads through nearly all of northern Africa. Relief is provided by the Atlas Mountains, which stretch through northwestern Africa. The highest peak is Mount Toubkal, which reaches a height of 4,165 metres (13,665 feet). Sudan is the largest African country.

ALGERIA

Adopted: 1962
Ratio: 2:3
Capital: Algiers
Independence (from France):
July 5, 1962
What it means: The colour green, and the crescent and star are Islamic symbols.

BENIN

Adopted: 1959
Ratio: 2:3
Capital: Porto-Novo
Independence (from France):
August 1, 1960
What it means: Features pan-African colours, symbolic of African unity.

BURKINA FASO

Adopted: 1984
Ratio: Approximately 2:3
Capital: Ouagadougou
Independence (from France):
August 5, 1960
What it means: The red is symbolic of the 1984 revolution.

CAMEROON

Adopted: 1975
Ratio: Approximately 2:3
Capital: Yaoundé
Independence (from UN trusteeship)
January 1, 1960
What it means: The central star symbolises national unity.

CAPE VERDE

Adopted: 1992
Ratio: 10:17
Capital: Praia
Independence (from Portugal):
July 5, 1975
What it means: The blue field and the stars represent the 10 main islands.

CÔTE D'IVOIRE

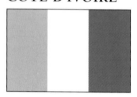

Adopted: 1959
Ratio: Approximately 2:3
Capital: Yamoussoukro
Independence (from France):
August 7, 1960
What it means: The flag symbolises dynamic growth, peace and hope.

EQUATORIAL GUINEA

Adopted: 1968
Ratio: Approximately 2:3
Capital: Malabo
Independence (from Spain):
October 12, 1968
What it means: The six stars represent the five principal islands and the mainland.

GABON

Adopted: 1960
Ratio: 3:4
Capital: Libreville
Independence (from France):
August 17, 1960
What it means: The green and yellow signify the country's natural wealth, while the blue represents the coast.

GAMBIA

Adopted: 1965
Ratio: 2:3
Capital: Banjul
Independence (from the United Kingdom): February 18, 1965
What it means: Red, blue and green represent Gambia's natural reserves.

GHANA

Adopted: 1957
Ratio: 2:3
Capital: Accra
Independence (from the United Kingdom): March 6, 1957
What it means: The black star stands for 'African freedom'.

GUINEA

Adopted: 1958
Ratio: 2:3
Capital: Conakry
Independence (from France):
October 2, 1958
What it means: The flag incorporates pan-African colours.

GUINEA-BISSAU

Adopted: 1973
Ratio: Approximately 1:2
Capital: Bissau
Independence (declared; from Portugal): September 24, 1973
What it means: The black star stands for the people's right to freedom.

LIBERIA

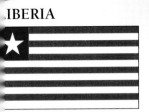

Adopted: 1847
Ratio: 10:19
Capital: Monrovia
Independence: July 26, 1847
What it means: The stripes are for the men who signed the Liberian Declaration of Independence.

MALI

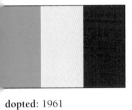

Adopted: 1961
Ratio: 2:3
Capital: Bamako
Independence (from France): September 22, 1960
What it means: The Mali flag uses Pan-African colours.

MAURITANIA

Adopted: 1959
Ratio: 2:3
Capital: Nouakchott
Independence (from France): November 28, 1960
What it means: The green field, the star and the crescent represent Islam.

MOROCCO

Adopted: 1915
Ratio: 2:3
Capital: Rabat
Independence (from France): March 2, 1956
What it means: Red is for the descendants of Prophet Muhammad.

NIGER

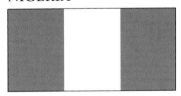

Adopted: 1959
Ratio: Approximately 6:7
Capital: Niamey
Independence (from France): August 3, 1960
What it means: The orange disc symbolises the sun.

NIGERIA

Adopted: 1960
Ratio: 1:2
Capital: Abuja
Independence (from the United Kingdom): October 1, 1960
What it means: White reminds of peace and unity, and green of the fertile land.

SÃO TOMÉ AND PRÍNCIPE

Adopted: 1975
Ratio: 1:2
Capital: São Tomé
Independence (from Portugal): July 12, 1975
What it means: The red triangle is a symbol for the freedom struggle.

SENEGAL

Adopted: 1960
Ratio: Approximately 2:3
Capital: Dakar
Independence (from France): April 4, 1960
What it means: The green star is symbolic of hope and unity.

SIERRA LEONE

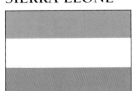

Adopted: 1961
Ratio: 2:3
Capital: Freetown
Independence (from the United Kingdom): April 27, 1961
What it means: Green stands for agricultural, white for unity and justice, and blue for the natural harbour at Freetown.

TOGO

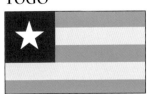

Adopted: 1960
Ratio: Approximately 3:5
Capital: Lomé
Independence (from French-administered UN trusteeship): April 27, 1960
What it means: The red field represents the values of love, loyalty and charity. It features the 'Star of Hope' and emphasises purity and national unity.

TUNISIA

Adopted: 1835
Ratio: 2:3
Capital: Tunis
Independence (from France): March 20, 1956
What it means: The red field is inspired by the national flag of Turkey.

EAST AFRICA

T he Great Rift Valley is a vast geological feature stretching from Ethiopia to Mozambique in East Africa. About 160 kilometres (100 miles) east of the East African Rift System (of which the Great Rift Valley is a branch) is Kilimanjaro, which is the highest point in Africa – its central cone reaches up to 5,895 metres (19,340 feet).

BURUNDI

Adopted: 1967
Ratio: 3:5
Capital: Bujumbura
Independence (from UN trusteeship under Belgian administration): July 1, 1962
What it means: The three stars represent the three main ethnic groups of the country – the Hutu, Tutsi and Twa.

Map labels

Tripoli
Cairo
LIBYA
EGYPT
CHAD
N'Djamena
ERITREA
Asmara
DJIBOUTI
Khartoum
Djibouti
SUDAN
SOMALIA
Addis Ababa
CENTRAL AFRICAN REPUBLIC
ETHIOPIA
Bangui
DEMOCRATIC REPUBLIC OF THE CONGO
UGANDA
KENYA
Mogadishu
Kampala
CONGO
Nairobi
Brazzaville
Kigali
RWANDA
Kinshasa
Bujumbura
Victoria
BURUNDI
SEYCHELLES

CHAD

Adopted: 1959
Ratio: 2:3
Capital: N'Djamena
Independence (from France): August 11, 1960
What it means: Uses the pan-African colours of red and yellow with the French tricolour's blue and red.

REPUBLIC OF THE CONGO

Adopted: 1958
Ratio: 2:3
Capital: Brazzaville
Independence (from France): August 15, 1960
What it means: Uses pan-African colours.

DEMOCRATIC REPUBLIC OF THE CONGO

Adopted: 1997
Ratio: 2:3
Capital: Kinshasa
Independence (from France): June 30, 1960
What it means: The six stars along the hoist were incorporated to represent the original provinces of Congo.

CENTRAL AFRICAN REPUBLIC

Adopted: 1958
Ratio: Approximately 3:5
Capital: Bangui
Independence (from the United Kingdom): August 13, 1960
What it means: The red stripe symbolises the bond between Africans and Europeans. The yellow star expresses hope for a bright future.

DJIBOUTI

Adopted: 1977
Ratio: Not specified
Capital: Djibouti
Independence (from France):
June 27, 1977
What it means: Blue represents the ssa people, and green the Afar people. The white triangle bears a red star for national unity.

ERITREA

Adopted: 1995
Ratio: 1:2
Capital: Asmara
Independence (from Ethiopia):
May 24, 1993
What it means: The green, blue and red are the party colours of the Eritrean People's Liberation Front (EPLF), who had led the independence struggle. The olive branch circled by a wreath was inspired by the flag of the United Nations and signify the country's autonomy.

ETHIOPIA

Adopted: 1996
Ratio: 1:2
Capital: Addis Ababa
Independence :
What it means: Pan-African colours are used. The star stands for unity among the Ethiopian nationalities.

KENYA

Adopted: 1963
Ratio: 2·3
Capital: Nairobi
Independence (from the United Kingdom): December 12, 1963
What it means: Black, red and green belonged to the Kenya African Union (KAU) party. White was added to represent the democractic party and national unity. The Masaishield with two crossed spears stand for national pride and tradition.

RWANDA

Adopted: 2001
Ratio: Approximately 2:3
Capital: Kigali
Independence (from Belgium-administered UN trusteeship):
July 1, 1962
What it means: Blue bears the message of happiness and peace. Yellow stands for economic progress, while green is symbolic of prosperity.

SEYCHELLES

Adopted: 1996
Ratio: 1:2
Capital: Victoria
Independence (from the United Kingdom): June 29, 1976
What it means: The red, white and green are the colors of the Seychelles People's United Party (SPUP). The blue and yellow are of the Democratic Party.

SOMALIA

Adopted: 1954
Ratio: 2:3
Capital: Mogadishu
Independence (from the United Kingdom and Italy): July 1, 1960
What it means: The blue field is inspired by the United Nations (UN) flag. The 'Star of Unity' is symbolic of the Somali people scattered across places such as Djibouti, Ethiopia and Kenya.

SUDAN, THE

Adopted: 1970
Ratio: 1:2
Capital: Khartoum
Independence (from Egypt and the United Kingdom): January 1, 1956
What it means: Red stands for socialism and progress, and white for peace and hope. Black recalls the name of the country (sudan is Arabic for 'black').

UGANDA

Adopted: 1962
Ratio: 2:3
Capital: Kampala
Independence (from the United Kingdom): October 9, 1962
What it means: The striped colours are from the tricolour of the Uganda People's Congress (UPC). The crested crane is the national symbol

EGYPT

Adopted: 1984
Ratio: 2:3
Capital: Cairo
Independence (from the United Kingdom): February 28, 1922
What it means: Pan-African colours are used. The coat of arms is the golden eagle of the 12th-century ruler Saladin, who fought in the Crusades.

LIBYA

Adopted: 1977
Ratio: 1:2
Capital: Tripoli
Independence (from Italy):
December 24, 1951
What it means: The only national flag to use a single colour.

CENTRAL AND SOUTHERN AFRICA

Central Africa lies across the Equator. The terrain consists of wide plateaus, which may reach a height of about 914 metres (3,000 feet) near the Angolan border. Central Africa's highest point is Margherita Peak – at 5,119 metres (16,795 feet). It is located on the eastern fringe of the Rift Valley.

Southern Africa too features a high interior plateau that consists of rolling grasslands. However, the monotony of the plateau is broken by the Kalahari desert and the Great Escarpment, a series of mountain ranges that run parallel to a narrow coastal strip. The Zambezi and the Limpopo are the largest rivers in the region.

ANGOLA

Adopted: 1975
Ratio: 2:3
Capital: Luanda
Independence (from Portugal): November 11, 1975
What it means: The machete and the cogwheel in the central yellow emblem stand for agriculture and industry, while the star is symbolic of progress. The red colour represents the blood shed during the freedom struggle and the black stands for Africa.

BOTSWANA

Adopted: 1966
Ratio: 2:3
Capital: Gaborone
Independence (from the United Kingdom): September 30, 1966
What it means: The blue background is symbolic of water and life, and the black-and-white centre, inspired by the coat of the national animal, zebra, signifies racial equality among the people.

COMOROS

Adopted: 2001 (current flag)
Ratio: 2:3
Capital: Moroni
Independence (from France): July 6, 1975
What it means: The crescent and stars are Islamic symbols. The four stars represent the main islands of the union.

LESOTHO

Adopted: 1987
Ratio: 9:14
Capital: Maseru
Independence (from the United Kingdom): October 4, 1966
What it means: The white triangle symbolises peace and features an outline of a shield with a spear and a traditional club. The green triangle stands for prosperity, while the blue band represents rain.

MADAGASCAR

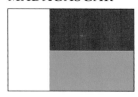

Adopted: 1958
Ratio: 2:3
Capital: Antananarivo
Independence (from France): June 26, 1960
What it means: Red and white are the traditional colours of Madagascar. Green is believed to recall the country's former peasant class (Hova).

MALAWI

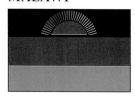

Adopted: 1964
Ratio: 2:3
Capital: Lilongwe
Independence (from France): July 6, 1964
What it means: Black (African heritage), red (blood of martyrs) and green (the land) are the colours of the Malawi Congress Party. The rising sun represents dawn of hope and freedom for the whole of Africa.

MAURITIUS

Adopted: 1968
Ratio: 2:3
Capital: Port Louis
Independence (from the United Kingdom): March 12, 1968
What it means: Red stands for the independence movement, blue for the Indian Ocean, yellow for the 'light of freedom shining over the island,' and green for the rich vegetation.

MOZAMBIQUE

Adopted: 1983
Ratio: Approximately 2:3
Capital: Maputo
Independence (from Portugal): June 25, 1975
What it means: The yellow star bears an open book (education) overlaid by a hoe (peasantry) and rifle (defence of the land).

SOUTH AFRICA

Adopted: 1994
Ratio: 2:3
Capital: Pretoria
Independence (from the United Kingdom): May 31, 1910; proclaimed a republic on May 31, 1961
What it means: The Y-shape symbolises 'converging of paths' and unification. The red, white and blue were taken from the colours of the 19th-century Boer Republics. The yellow, black and green are from the African National Congress (ANC) flag.

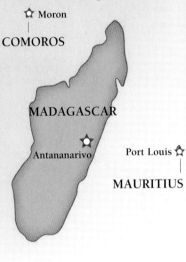

TANZANIA
☆ Dar es Salaam

☆ Luanda

ANGOLA

ZAMBIA
☆ Lusaka

MALAWI
☆ Lilongwe

MOZAMBIQUE

☆ Moron

COMOROS

MADAGASCAR
☆ Antananarivo

Port Louis ☆
MAURITIUS

NAMIBIA

NAMIBIA
☆ Windhoek

BOTSWANA

ZIMBABWE
☆ Harare

Adopted: 1990
Ratio: 2:3
Capital: Windhoek
Independence (from South African mandate): March 21, 1990
What it means: Blue, red and green were the flag colours of the South West Africa People's Organization (SWAPO), the group that liberated the country in 1990. The sun symbolises life and energy.

Gaborone ☆

☆ Pretoria

Maputo

Mbabane — SWAZILAND

LESOTHO
☆ Cairo

SOUTH AFRICA

SWAZILAND

Adopted: 1967
Ratio: 2:3
Capital: Mbabane
Independence (from the United Kingdom): September 6, 1968
What it means: The background is based on the flag that King Sobhuza II gave to the Swazi Pioneer Corps in 1941. The centered Swazi shield features two spears and a staff with hanging feather tassels of the widowbird.

ZAMBIA

Adopted: 1964
Ratio: 2:3
Capital: Lusaka
Independence (from the United Kingdom): October 24, 1964
What it means: The colours belonged to the United Nationalist Independent Party, the main political party during the time Zambia became independent. The eagle, taken from the national coat of arms, is symbolic of freedom and patriotism.

ZIMBABWE

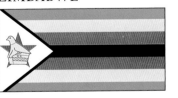

Adopted: 1980
Ratio: 1:2
Capital: Harare
Independence (from the United Kingdom): April 18, 1980
What it means: The Zimbabwe Bird is a national emblem. The triangle stands for peace and the red star denotes the government's socialist ideals.

TANZANIA

Adopted: 1964
Ratio: 2:3
Capital: Dar es Salaam
Independence (republic formed by union of Tanganyika and Zanzibar): April 26, 1964
What it means: The green and black were taken from the Tanganyika flag and represent the land and people of Tanzania. The blue, for the sea, came from the Zanzibar flag.

OCEANIA

Oceania is the name for a group of islands distributed across the Pacific Ocean. It includes over 10,000 islands and is normally divided into the regions of Australasia (Australia and New Zealand), Melanesia, Micronesia and Polynesia. Australia is the world's smallest continent as well as the sixth largest country. An isolated island, New Zealand is separated from its nearest neighbour, Australia, by more than 1,600 km (1,000 miles).

AUSTRALIA

Adopted: 1909
Ratio: 1:2
Capital: Canberra
Independence (federation of U.K. colonies): January 1, 1901
What it means: The Union Jack is featured on the upper hoist side, with the seven-pointed Commonwealth Star below. The five stars on the right half represent the Southern Cross constellation.

FIJI ISLANDS

Adopted: 1970
Ratio: 1:2
Capital: Suva
Independence (from the United Kingdom): October 10, 1970
What it means: The blue field is symbolic of the Pacific Ocean. The coat of arms displays a golden British lion, with the panels displaying sugar cane, a palm tree, bananas and the dove of peace.

KIRIBATI

Adopted: 1979
Ratio: 1:2
Capital: Bairiki
Independence (from the United Kingdom): July 12, 1979
What it means: The upper half shows a local frigate bird flying over the rising sun, as a symbol of strength and power at sea. The blue and white bands represent the Pacific Ocean.

MARSHALL ISLANDS

Adopted: 1979
Ratio: 10:19
Capital: Dalap-Uliga-Darrit (on Majuro Atoll)
Independence (from U.S.-administered UN trusteeship): October 21, 1986
What it means: The orange and white signify the country's parallel island chains. The 24-pointed star stands for as many districts of the islands.

MICRONESIA

Adopted: 1978
Ratio: 10:19
Capital: Palikir
Independence (from U.S.-administered UN trusteeship): November 3, 1986
What it means: The four stars stand for the four island groups in the country, centred on a blue field for the Pacific Ocean.

NAURU

Adopted: 1968
Ratio: 1:2
Capital: No official capital
Independence (from Australia-, New Zealand-, and U.K.-administered UN trusteeship): January 31, 1968
What it means: The yellow line represents the Equator, and the 12-pointed star stands for the 12 original tribes of Nauru.

NEW ZEALAND

Adopted: 1902
Ratio: 1:2
Capital: Wellington
Independence (from the United Kingdom): September 26, 1907
What it means: The stars represent the Southern Cross constellation.

PALAU

Adopted: 1981
Ratio: 5:8
Capital: Koror
Independence (from U.S.-administered UN trusteeship): October 1, 1994
What it means: Palauans regard the full moon, represented by the disc, auspicious for agriculture.

PAPUA NEW GUINEA

Adopted: 1971
Ratio: 3:4
Capital: Port Moresby
Independence (from Australia-administered UN trusteeship): September 16, 1975
What it means: The five stars stand for the Southern Cross, while the bird of-paradise is a local symbol. Red and black are native colours.

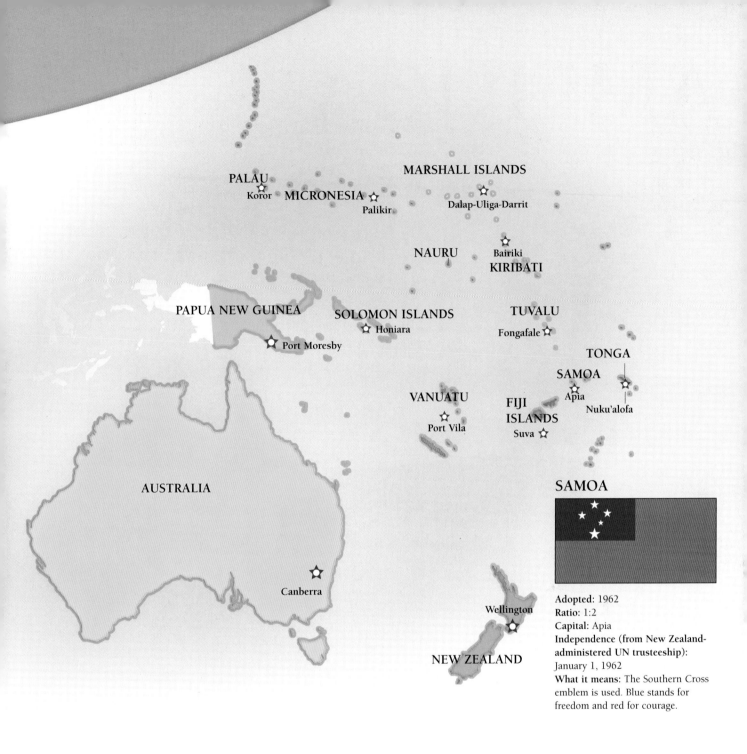

PALAU
Koror ☆   MICRONESIA ☆
              Palikir

MARSHALL ISLANDS
                ☆
        Dalap-Uliga-Darrit

NAURU   ☆ Bairiki
              KIRIBATI

PAPUA NEW GUINEA   SOLOMON ISLANDS   TUVALU
                        ☆ Honiara   Fongafale ☆
      ☆ Port Moresby

                                                    TONGA
                                        SAMOA
                              VANUATU   ☆ Apia
                          FIJI   Nuku'alofa
              ☆ Port Vila   ISLANDS
                              Suva ☆

AUSTRALIA

        ☆
        Canberra

        Wellington

              ☆

NEW ZEALAND

SAMOA

Adopted: 1962
Ratio: 1:2
Capital: Apia
Independence (from New Zealand-administered UN trusteeship): January 1, 1962
What it means: The Southern Cross emblem is used. Blue stands for freedom and red for courage.

SOLOMON ISLANDS

Adopted: 1977
Ratio: 1:2
Capital: Honiara
Independence (from the United Kingdom): July 7, 1978
What it means: The five white stars represent the country's original provinces. The blue triangle signifies water and the green, the land. The yellow stripe symbolises sunshine.

TONGA

Adopted: 1875
Ratio: 1:2
Capital: Nuku'alofa
Independence (from U.K. protectorate status): June 4, 1970
What it means: The red field is symbolic of the blood shed by Jesus on the cross. The cross stands as a symbol of Christianity, with the white representing purity.

TUVALU

Adopted: 1978
Ratio: 1:2
Capital: Fongafale (on Funafuti Atoll)
Independence (from the United Kingdom): October 1, 1978
What it means: The nine stars represent the nine islands that constitute the country.

VANUATU

Adopted: 1990
Ratio: 3:5
Capital: Port Vila
Independence (from France and the United Kingdom): July 30, 1980
What it means: The Y-shape represents the shape formed by the islands.

UNITED STATES OF
AMERICA

Alaska

Juneau

Hawaii

Honolulu

The United States is a federal republic made up of 50 states – 48 of these are connected into one continuous, compact piece. Alaska and Hawaii do not share their boundaries with any of the other states. Its total area of 9,529,063 sq km (3,679,192 square miles) makes the United States the world's fourth largest country (after Russia, Canada and China).

Alabama

Adopted: 1895
Ratio: 1:1
Capital: Montgomery
What it means: Based on the battle flag of the Confederate States during the Civil War.

Alaska

Adopted: 1959
Ratio: 2:3
Capital: Juneau
What it means: A 13-year-old boy, Benny Benson, designed this flag in 1926, depicting the North Star and the Ursa Major constellation.

Arizona

Adopted: 1913
Ratio: 2:3
Capital: Phoenix
What it means: The copper-coloured star represents the copper resources of Arizona.

Arkansas

Adopted: 1913
Ratio: 2:3
Capital: Little Rock
What it means: The diamond shape of the central white emblem symbolises the state's diamond production.

California

Adopted: 1911
Ratio: 2:3
Capital: Sacramento
What it means: The flag bearing a grizzly bear goes back to an 1846 local revolt.

Colorado

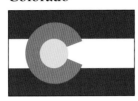

Adopted: 1911
Ratio: 2:3
Capital: Denver
What it means: The red 'C' recalls the Spanish word *colorado* ("red"), from which the name of the state originated.

Connecticut

Adopted: 1897
Ratio: 4:5
Capital: Hartford
What it means: The Latin inscription reads "He who transplanted still sustains us." This is based on a psalm.

Delaware

Adopted: 1913
Ratio: 3:4
Capital: Dover
What it means: The date beneath the coat of arms is when Delaware became the first state to formally approve the U.S. Constitution.

Florida

Adopted: 1900
Ratio: 2:3
Capital: Tallahassee
What it means: The flag recalls the Confederate flag of the Civil War. The state seal is at the centre.

Georgia

Adopted: 2003
Ratio: 2:3
Capital: Atlanta
What it means: The 13 stars around the state's coat of arms refer to Georgia as one of the 13 original colonies.

Hawaii

Adopted: 1845
Ratio: 1:2
Capital: Honolulu
What it means: The Union Jack can be traced to the year 1793, when a British army officer made gifted the flag to the Hawaiian king.

Idaho

Adopted: 1927
Ratio: 2:3
Capital: Boise
What it means: The flag is based on an earlier military banner.

Illinois

Adopted: 1915
Ratio: 3:5
Capital: Sacramento
What it means: The dates 1818 and 1868, respectively, stand for statehood and the first time the state seal was used.

Indiana

Adopted: 1917
Ratio: 2:3
Capital: Indianapolis
What it means: The 19 stars around the gold torch recall Indiana's status as the 19th state to join the Union.

Iowa

Adopted: 1921
Ratio: 2:3
Capital: Des Moines
What it means: The flag recalls the French tricolour – Iowa was once a part of French Louisiana.

Kansas

Adopted: 1925
Ratio: 3:5
Capital: Topeka
What it means: The sunflower was adopted as the state's floral emblem in 1903.

Kentucky

Adopted: 1918
Ratio: 2:3
Capital: Frankfort
What it means: The theme of national unity is reflected in the state seal

Louisiana

Adopted: 1912
Ratio: 2:3
Capital: Baton Rouge
What it means: The pelican represents the spirit of self-sacrifice.

Maine

Adopted: 1909
Ratio: 2:3
Capital: Augusta
What it means: The coat of arms depicts a farmer and a sailor representing the agricultural and shipbuilding industries. The Latin motto means, "I direct."

Maryland

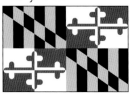

Adopted: 1904
Ratio: 2:3
Capital: Annapolis
What it means: The flag retains British heraldic symbols.

Massachusetts

Adopted: 1908
Ratio: 2:3
Capital: Boston
What it means: The Latin motto reads "By the sword we seek peace, but peace only under liberty." The coat of arms on a white background served many Massachusetts regiments.

Michigan

Adopted: 1911
Ratio: 2:3
Capital: Lansing
What it means: The state seal features the bald eagle, a shield, an elk and a moose. There are three Latin mottoes: "One out of many," "I will defend," and "If you seek a pleasant peninsula, look about you."

Minnesota

Adopted: 1893
Ratio: 7:11
Capital: St Paul
What it means: The state's motto, 'Star of the north', is shown on the red ribbon. Minnesota was the northernmost state in the Union before Alaska joined it.

Mississippi

Adopted: 1894
Ratio: 2:3
Capital: Jackson
What it means: The stripes retain the Stars and Bars of the Confederacy, while the canton features the Confederate Battle Flag.

Missouri

Adopted: 1913
Ratio: 10:17
Capital: Jefferson City
What it means: The Latin motto reads: "The welfare of the people shall be the supreme law."

Montana

Adopted: 1905
Ratio: 2:3
Capital: Helena
What it means: The state seal depicts the state's scenic landscape – the Rocky Mountains, the Great Falls, a river and forests. The plough, and the crossed pick and shovel are symbolic of agriculture and mining.

Nebraska

Adopted: 1963
Ratio: 3:5
Capital: Lincoln
What it means: The 1867 state seal is themed around Nebraska's agricultural and industrial development.

Nevada

Adopted: 1929
Ratio: 2:3
Capital: Carson City
What it means: The sagebrush is Nevada's state flower. The phrase 'Battle born' recalls Nevada's admission to the Union during the Civil War (1861-65).

New Hampshire

Adopted: 1909
Ratio: 2:3
Capital: Concord
What it means: The state seal was adopted in 1784 and it features the frigate *Raleigh*, which was built in 1776 and was one of the first ships in the nation's navy.

New Jersey

Adopted: 1896
Ratio: 2:3
Capital: Trenton
What it means: The field of buff (light tan) was taken from the uniform colour worn by New Jersey troops in the Revolutionary War (1775-83).

New Mexico

Adopted: 1925
Ratio: 2:3
Capital: Santa Fe
What it means: The sun symbol belonged to the Zia Pueblo Indians. Yellow and red were inspired by the flag of Spain, which controlled New Mexico until the beginning of the 19th century.

New York

Adopted: 1901
Ratio: 1:2
Capital: Albany
What it means: The coat of arms features a sun symbol and the two supporters of the shield – Liberty (on the left) and Justice.

North Carolina

Adopted: 1885
Ratio: 2:3
Capital: Raleigh
What it means: May 20, 1775, recalls the first meeting of North Carolina citizens proclaiming their freedom from Great Britain.

North Dakota

Adopted: 1911
Ratio: 2:3
Capital: Bismarck
What it means: The flag was earlier used by the state's military regiments.

Ohio

Adopted: 1902
Ratio: 5:8
Capital: Columbus
What it means: The swallow-tailed shape of the flag was probably inspired by a standard carried by the U.S. cavalry during the Civil War.

Oklahoma

Adopted: 1907
Ratio: 2:3
Capital: Oklahoma City
What it means: The bison-hide shield belongs to the Osage Indians. An olive branch and a Native American peace pipe are emblems of peace. The four small crosses are common motifs in Native American art and stand for high ideals.

Oregon

Adopted: 1925
Ratio: 3:5
Capital: Salem
What it means: The date commemorates Oregon's admission into the Union. Elements from the state seal are used. The reverse side depicts the beaver in golden yellow.

Pennsylvania

Adopted: 1907
Ratio: 2:3
Capital: Harrisburg
What it means: The coat of arms (from 1777) features the official seal of the William Penn family, the founders of Pennsylvania.

Rhode Island

Adopted: 1897
Ratio: 1:1
Capital: Providence
What it means: The centred anchor (symbolic of hope) has been the emblem of Rhode Island for centuries.

South Carolina

Adopted: 1861
Ratio: 2:3
Capital: Columbia
What it means: The palmetto is the state's official tree.

South Dakota

Adopted: 1963
Ratio: 3:5
Capital: Pierre
What it means: The state seal is depicted with the sun's rays around it. Among the elements featured in the seal are a farmer on his field, cattle, crops, a furnace and a steamship.

Tennessee

Adopted: 1905
Ratio: 3:5
Capital: Nashville
What it means: The design and colours are based on both the Confederate battle flag and the U.S. flag.

Texas

Adopted: 1839
Ratio: 2:3
Capital: Austin
What it means: The colours and the stripes are taken from the U.S. flag – blue for loyalty, white for strength, and red for bravery

Utah

Adopted: 1913
Ratio: 2:3
Capital: Salt Lake City
What it means: 1847 was the year when the first Mormon settlers came to Salt Lake City. 1896 marked Utah's joining the Union as the 45th state. The beehive is symbolic of industry. Sego lilies, the state flower, stand for peace.

Vermont

Adopted: 1923
Ratio: 3:5
Capital: Montpelier
What it means: The coat of arms pictures the Green Mountains in the background, with a large pine tree, a cow and sheaves of wheat in the foreground. A stag's head is at the crest.

Virginia

Adopted: 1861
Ratio: 7:11
Capital: Richmond
What it means: The state seal features a woman dressed as an ancient warrior, wearing a helmet and holding a spear and sword. She is standing over the figure of a tyrant lying on the ground. The Latin motto reads: "Thus always to tyrants."

Washington

Adopted: 1923
Ratio: 2:3
Capital: Olympia
What it means: The state seal bears the name of the state, the date of admission into the Union, and a bust of George Washington, the first president of U.S.A.

West Virginia

Adopted: 1929
Ratio: 10:19
Capital: Charleston
What it means: The seal has a farmer and a mountaineer standing on either side of a rock with the date when West Virginia was admitted into the Union

Wisconsin

Adopted: 1913
Ratio: 2:3
Capital: Madison
What it means: The date recalls the attainment of statehood. The U.S. motto "One out of many" and the national shield are inscribed at the centre.

Wyoming

Adopted: 1917
Ratio: 2:3
Capital: Cheyenne
What it means: The white bison carries the 1893 state seal. The seal depicts a rancher and a miner. The woman represents equal rights.

CANADA

The northernmost country in North America, Canada also makes up nearly two-fifths of the continent. The country occupies an area of 9,984,670 square kilometres (3,855,103 square miles).

Alberta

Adopted: 1968
Ratio: 1:2
Capital: Edmonton
What it means: The St George Cross recalls the region's English settlement.

British Columbia

Adopted: 1960
Ratio: 3:5
Capital: Victoria
What it means: Features an extended Union Jack in the upper half, with a golden crown at the centre.

Manitoba

Adopted: 1966
Ratio: 1:2
Capital: Winnipeg
What it means: The coat of arms bears a bison (a source of food and clothing) and the Cross of St George.

New Brunswick

Adopted: 1965
Ratio: 5:8
Capital: Fredericton
What it means: The golden lion in the upper red stripe is believed to recall the region's ties with England.

Newfoundland and Labrador

Adopted: 1980
Ratio: 1:2
Capital: Saint John's
What it means: The two red-outlined triangles represent the mainland and the islands.

Northwest Territories

Adopted: 1969
Ratio: 1:2
Capital: Yellowknife
What it means: Blue is symbolic of the skies and waters in the territory, and white of the ice and snow.

Nova Scotia

Adopted: 1929
Ratio: 3:4
Capital: Halifax
What it means: Based on the royal arms of Scotland and the Scottish St Andrew Cross (with the colours reversed).

Nunavut

Adopted: 1999
Ratio: 9:16
Capital: Iqaluit
What it means: The traditional *inuksuk* at the centre represents stone markers that guide people on land.

Ontario

Adopted: 1965
Ratio: 1:2
Capital: Toronto
What it means: This was the first flag in Canada to feature the maple leaf.

Prince Edward Island

Adopted: 1964
Ratio: 2:3
Capital: Charlottetown
What it means: Based on a banner featuring the 1905 coat of arms.

Quebec

Adopted: 1948
Ratio: 2:3
Capital: Québec City
What it means: Each of the quarters bear a fleur-de-lys (flowers), which has historic associations with France.

Saskatchewan

Adopted: 1962
Ratio: 1:2
Capital: Regina
What it means: The prairie lily is the official floral emblem of the province.

Yukon Territory

Adopted: 1967
Ratio: 1:2
Capital: Whitehorse
What it means: At the centre are the coat of arms and the territory's floral emblem.

UNITED KINGDOM

Great Britain – comprising England, Wales and Scotland – and Northern Island are together called the United Kingdom. It is an island country located off the northwestern coast of the European mainland. With the exception of the land border with the Republic of Ireland, the United Kingdom is surrounded by sea – the North Sea, the English Channel, the Celtic Sea, the Irish Sea and the Atlantic Ocean.

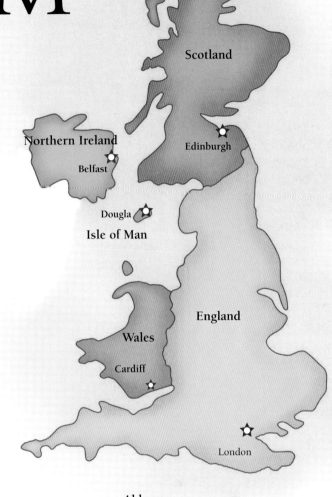

Scotland

Northern Ireland
Belfast

Edinburgh

Dougla
Isle of Man

England

Wales
Cardiff

London

Alderney
St Anne

Guernsey
St Peter Port   L'Ecluse ——— Sark

Jersey   St Helier

Alderney

Adopted: 1906
Ratio: 3:5
Capital: St Anne
What it means: Features the Cross of St George and the coat of arms.

England

Adopted: 1277
Ratio: 3:5
Capital: London
What it means: The Cross of St George is featured against a white field.

Guernsey

Adopted: 1962
Ratio: 2:3
Capital: St Peter Port
What it means: The gold cross sets it apart from the flag of England.

Isle of Man

Adopted in: 1971
Ratio: 1:2
Capital: Douglas
What it means: Features the symbol of *triskelion*, which is believed to be based on an ancient Sun symbol.

Jersey

Adopted: 1981
Ratio: 3:5
Capital: St Helier
What it means: The coat of arms and crown is featured at the top.

Northern Ireland

Adopted: 1973
Ratio: 1:2
Capital: Belfast
What it means: The Union Jack is currently used as the official flag.

Sark

Adopted: 1938
Ratio: 3:5
Capital: L'Ecluse
What it means: Incorporates the Cross of St George. The red canton features two yellow lions.

Scotland

Adopted: 1512
Ratio: 3:5
Capital: Edinburgh
What it means: The Cross of St Andrew is in honour of the patron saint of Scotland.

Wales

Adopted: 1959
Ratio: 3:5
Capital: Cardiff
What it means: The Red Dragon has long been an emblem for the Welsh people.

INTERNATIONAL FLAGS

Arab League

Features the emblem of the league, which currently comprises 22 Arab states.

Asean

The flag of the Association of Southeast Asian Nations represents the main colours of the flags of the 10 member nations.

Caricom

The yellow circle in the centre of the flag represents the sun, bearing the logo of the Caribbean Community and Common Market, founded in 1973.

CIS

The Commonwealth of Independent States is a confederation of 12 countries belonging to the former Soviet Union.

Commonwealth

The logo of the Commonwealth of Nations features the letter C about a representation of the globe.

European Union

The 12 gold stars symbolise the union of the peoples of European countries.

NATO

The North Atlantic Treaty Organization is an international defence alliance, meant chiefly for countries in Europe and North America.

OAS

The Organization of American States is an association of nearly all the independent countries in North America, Central America and South America.

Olympic Movement

The five interlocked rings were incorporated to represent the 'five parts of the world' in which the games were pursued actively.

OPEC

The Organization of Petroleum Exporting Countries was set up to coordinate petroleum-related policies of oil-producing nations.

Red Cross

The International Movement of the Red Cross and Red Crescent is a humanitarian agency. Its flag features the well known symbols of mercy and complete neutrality.

Pacific Community

The stars stand for the member countries.

United Nations

The flag depicts a map of the Earth flanked by two olive branches – an apt logo for a peacekeeping organisation.

African Union

The coat of arms is featured in the centre.

OIC

The flag of the Organization of the Islamic Conference features pan-Arab colours and the inscription 'Allahu Akbar', meaning 'God is great.'

SIGNAL FLAGS

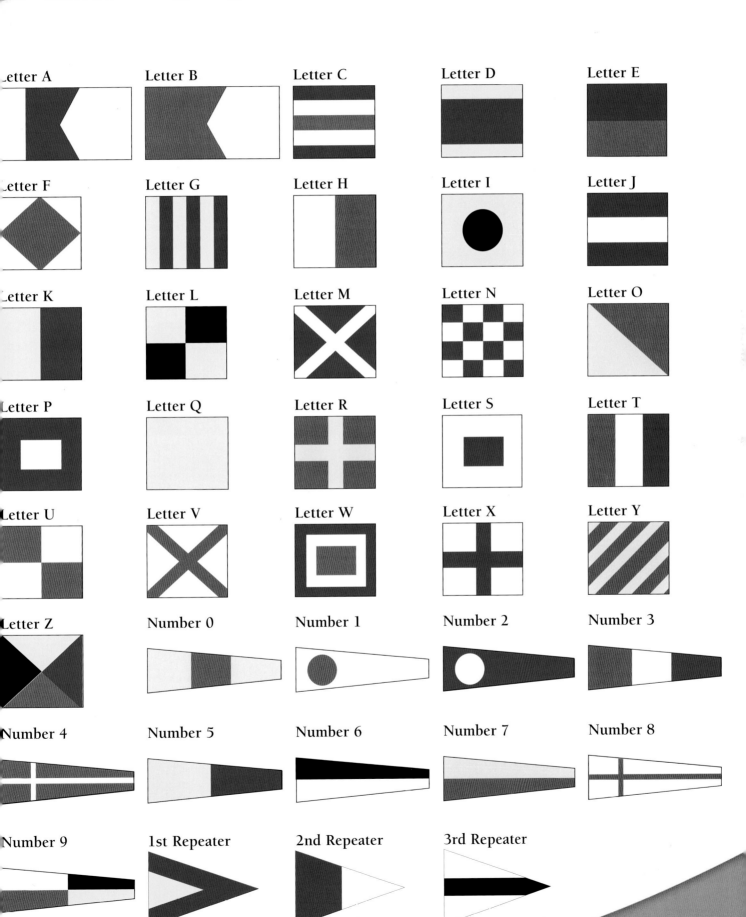

Letter A
Letter B
Letter C
Letter D
Letter E

Letter F
Letter G
Letter H
Letter I
Letter J

Letter K
Letter L
Letter M
Letter N
Letter O

Letter P
Letter Q
Letter R
Letter S
Letter T

Letter U
Letter V
Letter W
Letter X
Letter Y

Letter Z
Number 0
Number 1
Number 2
Number 3

Number 4
Number 5
Number 6
Number 7
Number 8

Number 9
1st Repeater
2nd Repeater
3rd Repeater

TYPES OF FLAGS

Match the given type of flags on this page with the specific flags on the opposite page. It will be interesting to see which shapes and designs are more commonly used!

1. BORDER

2. BICOLOUR

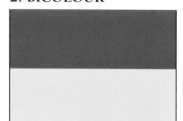

3. SALTIRE

4. TRICOLOUR

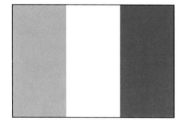

5. COUPED CROSS

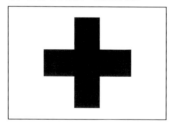

6. CROSS

7. FIMBRIATION

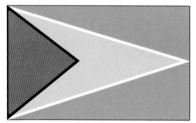

8. SCANDINAVIAN CROSS

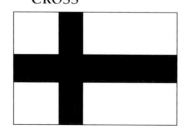

9. SERRATION

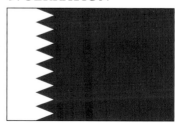

French Guina

Guyana

Austria

Maldives

Finland

Swiss Confederation

Letter V

Norway

Red Cross

Bahrain

Haiti

Mali

Scotland

Denmark

Florida

Grenada

Nigeria

Guernsey

Qatar

Indonesia

Poland

West Virginia

INDEX